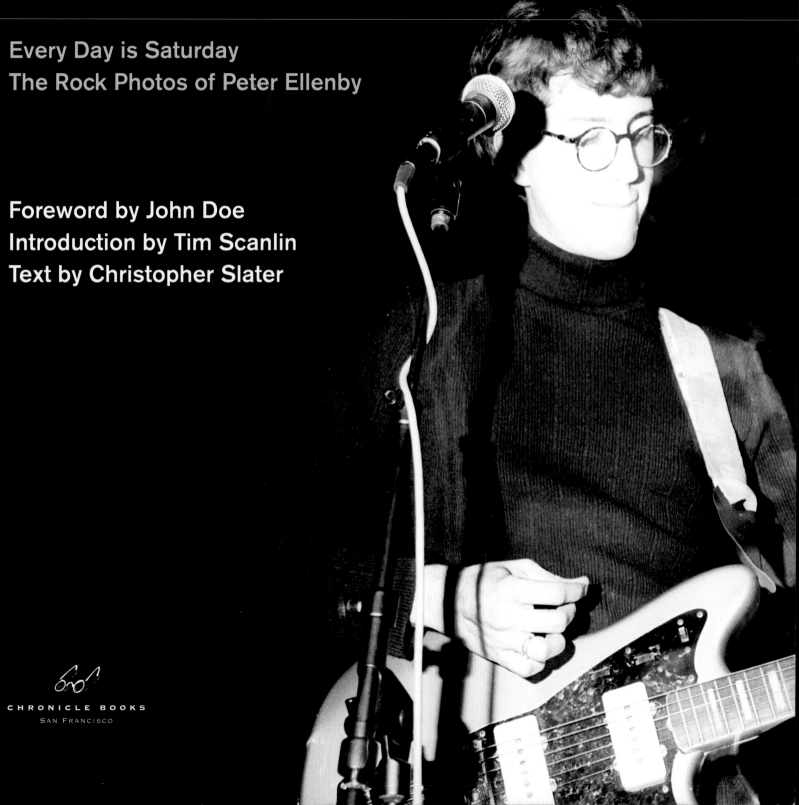

Every Day is Saturday
The Rock Photos of Peter Ellenby

Foreword by John Doe
Introduction by Tim Scanlin
Text by Christopher Slater

CHRONICLE BOOKS
SAN FRANCISCO

Library of Congress Cataloging-in-Publication Data
available.

ISBN-10: 0-8118-5397-7
ISBN-13: 978-0-8118-5397-2

Manufactured in China.

Designed by Jacob T. Gardner
Typeset in Berthold Akzidenz Grotesk

Distributed in Canada by Raincoast Books
9050 Shaughnessy Street
Vancouver, British Columbia V6P 6E5

10 9 8 7 6 5 4 3 2 1

Chronicle Books LLC
680 Second Street
San Francisco, California 94107

www.chroniclebooks.com

Dedication

This book is dedicated to my
amazing wife, Jeanné, to my entire
family, and all of my friends.
I couldn't have done it without
every last one of you.

In memory of my buddy Peeper.
Rest easy, friend.

Thanks to Parker and Amy at GIBBSMO Artist Management, for making this book happen; Alan Rapp and all at Chronicle Books, for believing in the project; Jacob Gardner, for the amazing design work; John Doe, Christopher Slater, Tim Scanlin, Eric Moffat, and Barry Simons; Kevin and the Noise Pop Festival; Jordan and Hari at Zeitgeist; Bob Reed (my rock-and-roll idol); Buzznet, *SnackCake!,* and *DIW*; Kathleen, Ramona, and everybody at the Bottom of the Hill; Thee Parkside (home of the magic bench); all the Noise Pop photographers, everybody who so generously lent a song to the CD, all the bands I've ever shot (thanks for the time and for the music), and all the labels and magazines who've used my work; and let's not forget "the kids."

This book is the culmination of twelve-plus years photographing musicians—mostly, but not exclusively by any means, indie bands. It's a collection of some of my favorite shots culled from thousands of frames, color and black-and-white, live and portraits. It's what I've been looking at and immersed in for the last decade (and more) of my life. It's the beer sweat and bruised toes from getting up to the front of a show to get a better shot, the smile I get when I see a print develop in the darkroom. It's the friends I've made through the music and documenting that music. It's a lot of hard work, but more importantly it's a lot of fun, captured on film.

The inspiration for this book came from the music and the musicians pictured within its covers. Its publication validates, even if just a tiny bit, the importance of these musicians and others like them and what their music means to people. There are bands and musicians in this book that few readers may have heard of, but the photographs are still telling and compelling and the bands' contributions no less important. The more well-known bands were captured mostly on their way up, when they were young and eager with very few barriers between them and my lens or, perhaps more significantly, between them and their musical expression. Just the way it should be.

—Peter Ellenby

There are so few photographers, especially in the world of "rock photography," that are worth more than one look. Peter Ellenby qualifies as one of those few.

In this specific world, the atmosphere can become so self-conscious, so quickly, everyone is constantly on guard. This is a huge hurdle to overcome. One reason to venture out of doors is to distract the poor subjects as they increasingly look like little bunnies in the high beams. Then there's the "I'm-lookin'-tough-so-you-won't-see-how-scared-shitless-I-am" look, which sometimes includes railroad tracks. Within any landscape there are moments of truth, but they are so masked and faded that all one sees are the ghosts of the figures that once floated in front of the lens.

Only in rare cases does a zone of comfort and ease inside one's skin exist before the camera. This is a bubble that Ellenby seems to bring to every shoot. He gives a confidence that you actually belong in front of his lens and that you may, in the future, amount to something more than a beggar, bum, or musician. It's clearly evident that the low-key atmosphere and familiar surroundings offer the subjects and viewer a precious window to a moment in time. There is nakedness and honesty and a chance to see the person inside the subject in all of Ellenby's frames. This also allows any of his subjects an opportunity to project a persona or play a part for the camera.

Then there was the first time I met and worked with Peter. Our first location, outside Bakersfield by the Kern River, where Mexican families wade in the hip-deep run-off from the winter snows, also happens to be a prime make-out spot under Highway 99. Bras, panties, boxers, and assorted pieces of clothing littered the rocks on which we shot. The pastoral river in the background of our shot was a total lie, but we knew where we were.

Then off to the rarely used '50s movie theater in downtown Bakersfield. Here we portrayed or projected a sort of carny huckster, with Peter using fish-eye lenses and blowing out the black and white. The comfort and immediate connection I felt told me this session would be worth the adventure. I drove back to the mountains while Peter and his assistant/friend stayed in Bakersfield to visit Trout's, the best remaining old-time honky-tonk in Oildale. This was one of the joints where Merle Haggard and Buck Owens refined the "Bakersfield sound." Apparently Peter and friend drank to excess, almost got whupped, and the next morning were so hung-over they filled their gas tank with diesel fuel, which they had to siphon by sucking on a piece of garden hose, getting a mouthful in the process—clearly an unjust punishment to endure with a brain-busting hangover.

One of the most lasting contributions made by Ellenby and his photos is his documentation of San Francisco and the era in which his pictures were taken. There is little or no romanticizing in the starkness of the cityscapes, and because of this they also have a timelessness that transcends today. In the future, people will view these photos and think, "Man, San Francisco back then must've been such a hip place to be in a band." Certainly it was, and we have Peter Ellenby to thank for letting us see it.

John Doe is a founding member of X and of The Knitters, and has released seven solo albums. Mr. Doe has also appeared in more than forty films and several television programs.

John Doe 1998

Introduction by Tim Scanlin

A pint in one hand and a camera in the other. That's my enduring mental image of Peter Ellenby.

While he is many other things— a cutup, a gentleman, a loyal friend—he is the undisputed master of the one-handed flick 'n' click, a Pabst-fueled Pollockesque technique perfected in the beer-soaked expanse between stage and fans, usually under fire by very high-decibel levels.

These days Peter is a celebrity in the world of independent music. What Charles Peterson was to Seattle, Peter Ellenby is to San Francisco, and beyond. But it wasn't always thus. Sit down and I'll tell you a story . . .

In late 1995, I was drowning in a sea of postgrad depression. Desperate for a diversion from my day job at the University of California, I decided to start a zine. It would be called—what else??— *SnackCake!,* and its mission would be to cover great bands that no one knew about. While frustrated publicists rejoiced, my parents seriously considered an intervention.

I shanghaied a few friends and we cobbled together the first issue, a thirty-two-page monument to youthful enthusiasm and naivete that came out in January of 1996. A couple more issues followed. The magazine was gaining steam and we were pleased with ourselves. But in the back of my mind, I knew something was missing. We needed a look, an aesthetic that set us apart. We needed something that was ours.

Across the Bay, Peter Ellenby could usually be found snapping away at his local haunt, a small club nestled at the bottom of Potrero Hill called, appropriately enough, Bottom of the Hill.

Knowing of my predicament, someone suggested that I talk to Ellenby. I introduced myself via email and we arranged to meet at a Meices show at the Bottom during the fourth annual Noise Pop Festival. Noise Pop was the brainchild of another Bay Area music fanatic, Kevin Arnold. Kevin had launched the fest three years previously and it lived up to its billing big-time, featuring the cream of SF's fuzzy melodic underground, bands like ¡Carlos!,

Corduroy, and the very aptly named Overwhelming Colorfast.

I was immediately struck by how down-to-earth Peter was. A genuinely nice guy, I thought, with an impressive camera to match. We talked a bit and he agreed to contribute some photos to the next issue of *SnackCake!*

Having never actually seen Peter's work, I had no idea what to expect. At this time in the magazine's gestation, I was settling for anything that was in focus. In short, my expectations were slung lower than Joe Meice's guitar.

When I saw Peter's photos, I was astonished. They exuded a vibrancy and skill that I'd never seen in photographs before, or since. The black-and-white shots before me not only chronicled (in focus!) the rockage that I had witnessed standing in the crowd two weeks before, they somehow captured the energy of the moment, the feeling of being there. Technically, I knew what was up: Peter had left the shutter on his Minolta open just long enough to keep things in focus, while also creating a ghostly backdrop of blurred guitars and elongated chrome reflections that looked like a child's finger painting (the fish-eye lens—one of Peter's favorite toys—further enhanced this effect). However, the impact—the feeling you got when confronted with these pictures—was anything but cerebral or calculated. Staring down at the photos, I wondered how someone this talented could be so relatively unknown. The

answer, I would eventually discover, is that Peter is a true artist for whom the work is paramount, with the rewards and acclaim coming a distant second.

I knew instantly that *Snack-Cake!* had found the thing that would set it apart, and I was ecstatic. I felt like I had a big secret, one that I couldn't wait to share with the rest of the world.

Summoning as much cool detachment as my giddiness would allow, I informed Peter that his photos were satisfactory, and asked if he might like to take on some new assignments for the magazine. He accepted and immediately got to work, shooting the Supersuckers, Swell, Jawbox, and You Am I in quick succession. Everything was amazing, and my fascination and admiration grew in equal measure. In the resulting issue, Peter was christened photo editor and chosen as our *Snack-Cake!* Superstar for work above and beyond the call of duty. We also gave him a free ad. Beneath a drawing of him chomping on a cigar and wearing X-ray specs was the line, "These labels have actually paid me for my work! You can too!" It was classic Peter.

Things kept moving. The glossy (albeit black-and-white) cover of our first issue of 1997 featured Peter's photo of hometown heroes Overwhelming Colorfast. For the next issue, Peter and my coeditor Rick Stone flew to Seattle to interview and photograph Noise Pop favorites the Fastbacks. Peter's photos captured all of the band's humor and energy, and I was overjoyed. One of those shots became our first color cover. More classic covers followed: Built to Spill post–sound check at Slim's, the Poster Children demolishing Bottom of the Hill, Luna being nonchalant outside the Fillmore, a stunning black-and-white portrait of John Doe under a bridge in Bakersfield.

The magazine was now distributed internationally, and we began publishing the official program guide of the Noise Pop Festival. Our stature was growing, largely because of Peter's amazing photographs. Suddenly, we gained entrée to a cavalcade of artists we'd only dreamed of covering: Supergrass, Ween, the Chills, Yo La Tengo, Old 97's, the Melvins

Superchunk, Modest Mouse, Mike Watt, Spiritualized, the Jesus Lizard, Rocket from the Crypt, and, my idols, X. Peter even got the opportunity to interview and photograph his heroes Run-DMC and, in a truly surreal exchange, asked about their favorite snack cakes.

While all of this star power was intoxicating and helped sell magazines, it was Peter's devotion to the people closest to him—local artists—that really floored me and made me understand the depth of his artistic integrity. San Francisco has always been a hotbed of talent, and in the last decade of the millennium the scene was booming. Peter was out every night of the week almost single-handedly chronicling an entire era of San Francisco rock. The bands were legion. Swell, American Music Club, Jawbreaker, Creeper Lagoon, Richard Buckner, Overwhelming Colorfast, !Carlosi, The Meices, Oranger, Beulah, MK Ultra, Kingdom First, Package, Hugh, Engine 88, Bracket. Whether he was shooting for the magazine or for a band's press kit, Peter always gave his peers—his friends— 100 percent of his talents.

By the dawn of 1999, I was a shell of a person. My magazine duties, combined with being in a touring band and cultivating a relationship with my future wife, had all conspired to wear me down to the nub. When a blood vessel in my eye burst due to stress and lack of sleep, I knew something had to give. I decided to fold the magazine.

Peter was understanding, but resolute in his desire to carry on. When *SnackCake!* managing editor Mike Cloward and Peter decided to pick up the mantle and launch their own magazine, *Devil in the Woods,* an outlet for Peter's work was assured. I felt very relieved.

Our last cover was a stark portrait of one of my heroes, Bob Mould of Hüsker Dü and Sugar. Once again Peter seemed to perfectly capture the essence of his subject, and it was a fitting closure to our time working together.

I consider Peter to be one of the most gifted artists I've ever come across, from recent years or otherwise. His photos exhibit that rarest of qualities: the ability to capture lightning in a bottle, time after time, and make it look totally effortless. That's no small feat with a pint in your hand.

Tim Scanlin was the publisher and editor-in-chief of Berkeley-based *SnackCake!* magazine. He was and remains a member of Actionslacks.

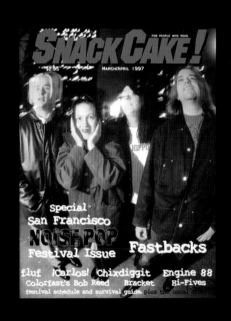

Death Cab for Cutie 1998

Peter has that rare ability to make a band actually enjoy having their photos taken. We've had our photos taken by Peter on many occasions, and he has proven to be one of the only photographers that can make you forget he's got a camera in his hand.

—Ben Gibbard, lead singer, Death Cab for Cutie

Thank Dizzy

In 1975, Dizzy Gillespie walked into a multipurpose room stuffed with children in a Palo Alto, California, elementary school. When he puffed his trademark cheeks and blew into his horn, seven-year-old Peter Ellenby had an epiphany. "It was just so amazing, so mind-blowing to see someone take a piece of metal and create such amazing music from it," Ellenby recalls. It's remarkable that one of the greatest jazz trumpeters the world has ever seen would play at an elementary school, but not so surprising that a young boy would get turned on by the experience. "I didn't even know who he was. He was just this guy who was going to come and play trumpet for us."

Peter Ellenby was born in 1968 in London, England, to artist mother Gillian and computer-scientist father John. The family, including older brother Tom, moved immediately thereafter to Edinburgh, Scotland, where they stayed until Peter turned six. Then, in 1974, John Ellenby packed the family off to what would become Silicon Valley to design computers, setting Peter up for the elementary-school assembly he would never forget. "I just had this humongous grin on my face—I just could not stop grinning," says Ellenby. "I think that's when I got hooked on music." A few years later, he started his record collection. "When I was in fourth grade, I bought my first records by myself. My parents had bought me Beach Boys records,

Goofy Greats—you know, all that stuff . . . 'The Red Baron.' Anyway, I went and bought *Van Halen* and *Cheap Trick at Budokan*."

Yet while young Peter may have been turned on to music by Mr. John Birks Gillespie, he learned photography at home. "My dad's a really good amateur photographer," explains Ellenby, "so there were always cameras around the house. My mom had a Nikon and she wouldn't care if I wanted to take pictures with it. I had a little 110 camera. For a while I got into making animated films with a Super-8 camera, like claymation. In seventh grade we made this brilliant dinosaur movie. I don't know—I've just always loved cameras, and it's always been part of what I've done. I've always taken pictures."

After taking a couple of black-and-white photography classes in high school, Ellenby decided to try a color class in college at Chico State. "I kinda got a kick in the pants from my teacher," he recalls. "I took this technically beautiful picture. It was a picture of a bluff up in Chico with a big cloud above it. It was really nice, the colors were nice, the time of day was nice. But my teacher was like, 'This is a really good photograph. But you know what? It's boring. It's just boring.' And I thought, you know, he's totally fucking right. From then on I didn't want to take boring pictures. I just wanted to take weird pictures. And I really thank him for that, because a lot of teachers, I think—and I've never been to art school, so I don't know what it's like there—but I think there's way too much analysis. He just told it so simply."

Actionslacks 1998

Appleseed Cast 2002

John Vanderslice 2002

Engine 88 1996

Beulah 1998

Beulah 2003

The Anniversary 2000

Her Space Holiday 2001

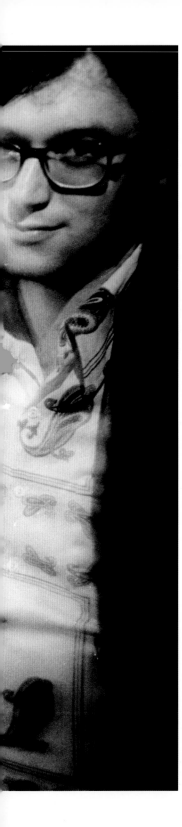

Jimmy Eat World 2001

The Pattern 2001

Indie

Sea changes in rock music have always been affected by upstart kids, and indie rock is no exception. The kids who made music, both noisy and gentle, in basements and garages, released their hiss-laden tapes into the world, often submitting them to tiny college radio stations. Punk rock had lain in wait for this generation; they discovered it as they grew up, and found it to be refreshingly sincere, even if it was a big "fuck you" to authority. Credibility—a.k.a. indie cred—could be gained by following punk rock, DIY ideals. Not that all its adherents really lived (or lived up to) this—and, in a case of irony doubling back on itself, plenty of people mocked indie conventions even as they continued to live within them, whether by accident or by choice. The chorus of the Actionslacks song "Self-Conscious Spiel," for instance, has singer Tim Scanlin snarling, "We've got so much cred, you know it's all I can do to get out of bed."

The do-it-yourself ethic was born out of the desire to create something that wasn't tainted by Reaganomics, corporate motivations, and marketing goals. Making a record on a cheap four-track in your bedroom was about as authentic as you could get, even if the end result sounded like it was recorded under a blanket and played through a coffee can. Indeed, this became an identifiable sound in its own right, the hallmark of authenticity. Lo-fi was the only way to go because that's all anyone could afford. Yet it quickly came to stand for more than that, as a reaction against the slick commercial pap that made the Billboard Top 20 every week. Lo-fi began as pragmatism—the only affordable way to get one's music

rapidly into an aesthetic that represented sincerity, independence, and a certain amount of cynicism.

Today, any overloaded self-consciousness has mostly worn off. "Indie rock" is now a pretty slippery term. Death Cab for Cutie signs to Atlantic and no one gets particularly bent out of shape about it, for instance. Are they still indie? Furthermore, hip-hop's groundbreaking sampling of anything and everything, plus the explosion of electronic music, has opened the ears of musicians and songwriters to mash-ups, collaborations, hybrid genres, and any other combinations they care to dream up. Independent music has reasserted itself in popular culture and in the open market, and only the crabbiest armchair critic would argue that it's for the worse.

Ellenby has some thoughts on what indie is all about:

Indie rock to me is music that, as the name says, is a totally independent creation of the songwriter or band. You can be on a major label and still make indie rock as long as the label doesn't have their nose up your ass while you write and record. It's all about the process, being driven by the need to create music, not to create money. Not to have a Top 40 hit, but to have something you can listen to and play for your friends and know that it represents you and you alone. I'd like to think my photography has the same sort of motivation and appeal behind it. I kind of get bummed out when people I shoot try to tell me what to do. Why not just go to the Sears portrait studio or take it yourself if you already know what you want? I want people to use me for my vision.

Oranger 1998

. . . And You Will Know Us by the Trail of Dead 2002

. . . And You Will Know Us by the Trail of Dead 2001

Death Cab for Cutie 1998

Death Cab for Cutie 2000

The Donnas 2000

Earlimart 1999

Fastbacks 1997

Modest Mouse 2003

Before the boom years, Peter Ellenby was a young man looking for a way to get into music. Frankly, he only pursued music photography after he figured out how much he loved it:

I was a band manager for a while, which is kind of how I got into music photography. The band would just have me take all the pictures because I was a pretty decent photographer. When we'd tour, we'd take pictures of the band in the desert. It was this band called the Rise. Never really got anywhere, but we went on tour a few times, and had a lot of fun for young kids, saw pretty much every western state in the country, lived on $5 a day. But when the band had broken up, I thought, that job kinda sucked—being a band manager and a road manager and a roadie and the guitar tech. It's really a pain in the ass dealing with club owners. "Hey man, the fucking contract says you're supposed to get us a $10 pizza." Then they stiff you! Arguing about stuff like that was not for me. But the photography part was really fun. It was my chance to be creative.

instead of changing guitar strings or making sure I had the delay set to the right patch for the guitar solos. So I had some other friends who were in this heavy metal band called Epidemic, and they had just signed a deal with Metal Blade Records. And I asked for a chance to take their pictures, and they agreed. I actually took one of my—still to this day—one of my favorite pictures. We were out at night, up in the fog on Skyline Boulevard in San Mateo. It was a fish-eye shot, and I took the flash off the camera and was just popping them with the flash at different angles, and it just turned out to be the most eerie photo ever. And they were a metal band, so it was totally perfect. That was on the inside of their CD insert, and it looked so great and it was such a thrill to have your picture out there, I guess it was kind of like, I dunno, like a drug, kinda.

Man, I just wanted to keep doing this because it felt so damn good.

Epidemic 1991

After college, Peter languished in East Palo Alto for a while, taking pictures and working as a barista and coffee roaster at a coffee shop, where he displayed portraits of regulars and staff members on the walls in a show dubbed "Espresso Expressions" by the shop's manager. A couple of years of Palo Alto and Ellenby, like a million other twentysomethings, decided San Francisco was the place to be. Through the classifieds he found a live/work space with a darkroom in Dogpatch, a neighborhood of warehouses, defunct rail lines, and dry-dock stations along the eastern piers, and moved in two days later. It turns out that moving to this apartment was probably the thing that really kick-started Ellenby's immersion in shooting live music. He knew that a new rock club, the Bottom of the Hill, was about five blocks away, and he discovered that they didn't mind if he brought his camera to shows.

Ellenby was pretty lucky to find the apartment he did, all things considered. "Bottom of the Hill is he best rock-and-roll nightclub, maybe in the whole country—my opinion—and I could just go down there, walk there with my camera," he explains.

As Ramona Downey and Kathleen Owen, two of the three owners of the Bottom of the Hill, will attest, the walk-in convenience enjoyed by Ellenby is rare. Downey—a charming brunette who booked bands at the Blue Lamp in San Francisco's Tenderloin district before working at, and eventually buying, the Bottom of the Hill—says, "There's a perception that Bottom of the Hill is too far away [from the city center]." "But we've always had parking," quips the vivacious Owen, with an easy laugh. The women frequently finish each other's thoughts. "There's zero walk-in business," Owen explains, "because there's no sensible reason anyone would walk around [this part of] Potrero Hill after bedtime." Downey is unequivocal. "If the shows don't draw, there's no business."

Yet Ellenby would walk over frequently, whether or not he knew the band who was playing, and bring his camera. Owen attributes the walking as much to Ellenby's nature as his proximity to the club. "Peter walks all the time, everywhere," she says. Downey laughs and fills in the punchline: "It means he can drink as much as he wants."

"At first I'd have to pay to get in," says Ellenby, "and then I would take photos of random shows whoever was playing, I'd just shoot it." Ellenby was happy to pay his way, too. "Peter never asked for special treatment or anything like that—free entry, guest list, free drinks, et cetera," continues Downey. "He came over to see shows and shoot pictures." After a year or so of shooting prolifically at the club, one day he surprised Downey and Owen with a large package. "They started letting me in for free because I started giving them prints," Ellenby says.

"It's great that we have an archive," says Owen. "He's been like the house photographer for the last ten years." Which suits Ellenby just fine: "The club loves it when I take pictures. They get a permanent record of the shows and they can put them on their

wall. I started giving them portraits too. It's really cool to go to the club and see my work on the walls. I'm not there every night, but I kind of am. People are looking at my work."

Poster Children 1997

Oranger 2001

Overwhelming Colorfast 1995

Zen Guerrilla 2001

The Pattern 2001

Hey Mercedes 2001

Creeper Lagoon 2001

Noise Pop

If proximity to Bottom of the Hill was one major building block for Ellenby's career in music photography, the other one was undoubtedly the Noise Pop Festival. Kevin Arnold, founder and currently the CEO of IODA, an Internet music distribution company, says he started the Noise Pop Festival in 1993 because he wanted to see all of his favorite local bands play on the same bill. The Texas native (with no accent to speak of) wrangled Overwhelming Colorfast, the Meices, Corduroy, ¡Carlos!, and

Bitchcraft to play at the Kennel Club, a larger room than any of the bands usually headlined. Bob Reed, the curly-haired principal architect of Overwhelming Colorfast who currently plays guitar in Oranger, has a slightly different take. "Kevin Arnold was Overwhelming Colorfast's tour manager and booker," he explains, chuckling. "I guess you could say that Kevin was basically creating a festival to promote the band that he was managing." Either way, Arnold dubbed the show Noise Pop and called it a festival "for marketing reasons. You know, 'It'll be this big event for $5, it'll be a festival!'" It worked, too. "I thought, maybe we'll have a good three, four hundred people there," remembers Arnold, a smile breaking out on his boyish face. "In the end, I think we actually sold something like eight hundred tickets to the show. It was massively oversold—it was really, really fucking packed. I don't think anybody expected it to do near as good as it did, and it was the raddest thing."

Arnold wasn't the only one excited about the lineup. To Ellenby, Noise Pop was the perfect show: "I loved all the bands—Overwhelming Color-fast, my favorite band of all time, headlined. I was totally going nuts, I had the greatest time. Unfortunately I didn't take any pictures, but I don't know whose fault that was."

The bands loved the show, too, and the following year they started asking Arnold months ahead of time whether he'd be doing it again. Regrettably for Ellenby, he was out of the country when Noise Pop 2 happened, but there was no way he was going to miss the third one. And he wouldn't just be a fan in the crowd, either.

"So I'm in San Francisco," Ellenby recalls, "and my friend Alistair calls me and says, 'Hey, we're starting

an online magazine called Buzznet."
I thought, 'online,' what the fuck
is that? [Laughs] This was a long
time ago." He began shooting
photos for the Web site, covering
music and cultural events. "So
then one day Alistair says, 'Hey,
the Noise Pop Festival is coming
up. We're going to cover it for
them. Can you shoot it?' Hell yeah!

"I was assigned to shoot every
band of every show," he continues.
"But there were no overlapping
shows back then, so it was just
like, show show show show. You
could go to every single show and
see every single band, and it was

so great. It was like a roving party.
Whatever club it was in, it was
almost the same crowd. Half the
crowd had been at every show.
And it was super fun."

Arnold recalls how great it was
to work with Ellenby: "Peter was
a friend by that point. Maybe we
called him the 'unofficial' Noise
Pop photographer for a while,
and then eventually he was the
official Noise Pop photographer.
He just basically did it, at first,
and it was like, 'Oh awesome, we
should put these pictures on the
Web site,' and he was always into
that. He'd go right home and process and print them." When the
festival began to stage simultan-
eous shows at different venues,
Ellenby cut back on his own

shooting to coordinate the other photographers.

All this photography was happening, but the question was, how to get them seen by people? "We wanted it to be real time—this is happening now, let's put it up now," says Ellenby. "Some writer would write a little thing about each show, and I would come home after the show, process the film in the darkroom, wake up, print, then take the prints down to *Buzznet.* They would scan them—I

and take the PC to the next show, so people at that show would be looking at the Web site going, 'Oh my God, I was at that show last night.' This was way before digital cameras and photo blogging and whatever's going on now."

"I think when Noise Pop started," observes San Francisco author and musician Beth Lisick, "that was really smart. Somebody identified that something was happening and they did something about it. They made a festival out of that. There were a lot of people playing music at the time, but it seemed like Noise Pop made this cohesion happen. It happened at the perfect time; there were all of these elements, and making a festival out of it really made it come together and be something that people could identify a lot better." Something was happening, though word of mouth could only do so much to nurture a music scene. Noise Pop's exponential growth in subsequent years attests to its musical zeitgeist.

Noise Pop and the success of Ellenby's photographs opened up a much larger world for him, both professionally and personally: "I really met a whole lot of people. We had so much fun doing this thing. I mean, it was totally exhausting, but it was the catalyst. I realized, this is exactly what I want to be doing. Going to the shows, seeing amazing bands, finding new amazing bands, meeting new amazing people, meeting my wife. It's not just about music and photography—it's about friendship and all this other stuff. And it all started that weekend. I think it was four days. You know, like, when you hear a song and you say, 'I've been waiting for this song forever.' Or when you meet your soul mate, it's like, 'This is what I love.' It's so great to finally find that."

Kevin Arnold, Noise Pop Founder 1998

¡Carlos! 1997

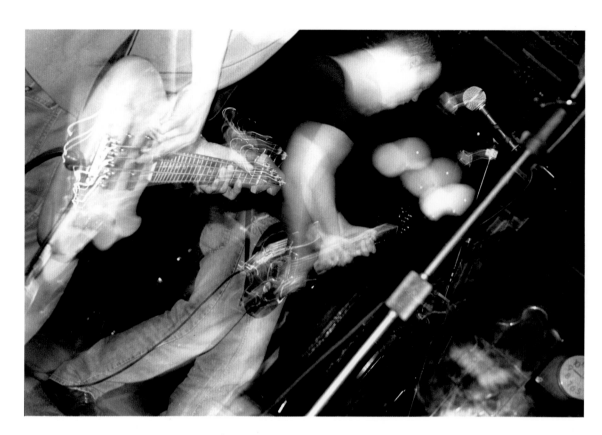

Overwhelming Colorfast 1995

Overwhelming Colorfast 1996

Aislers Set 2000

Fastbacks 2002

Flaming Boom Boxes

Peter on the Flaming Lips Boom Box Experiment #4 that took place during the 1998 Noise Pop Festival:

The Boom Box Experiment was one of the most amazing and mind-blowing shows I have ever experienced. The mad geniuses who call themselves the Flaming Lips got together forty or so old boom boxes. They created individual audiotapes for each of the boxes and then invited audience members to jump on stage and operate the boxes. The Lips conducted the boom-box operators to start, stop, and adjust the volume on their cues, each section of operators being given different directions. The boxes were all hooked to a sound board where they were mixed together and the result was fed to the crowd through an eight- or sixteen-speaker sound system. The resulting music was so amazing and unique that everybody in the audience was just blown away. You can see it in the faces of the crowd, the boom-box operators, and the band when you look at the photos from that night. People were just floored.

The Flaming Lips 1998

The Flaming Lips 1998

Devil in the Woods

When the staffers at *SnackCake!* decided enough was enough, the magazine dissolved and another came forward to take its place. *Devil in the Woods,* founded by Mike Cloward and Ellenby, and published by Cloward's record label of the same name, decided to set its sights on a national market. After Cloward assigned stories to his writers, he hired Marc Hawthorne to edit. Ellenby was already the photo editor, and Hawthorne remembers meeting him at his house for the first production meeting. He said one of his major concerns was Peter's cat, Peeper. "I remember his cat being really mean to everybody but Peter," says Hawthorne.

Unlike many editors, Hawthorne prized the images in *DIW* as highly as the text. "As important as I felt the words were in *DIW,*" he affirms, "the photos had to be just as strong. It was really important to me that it looked really good. And I wanted to stay away from us using any promo shots at all. If I could make it 100 percent our own stuff, I would." It turns out that maintaining such high quality became a financial struggle for the start-up magazine. "As our paper stock got better and we went to full color," says Hawthorne, "we were still reaching for that goal of having all our own pictures in the magazine, and Peter was blowing our budget out. We were running up a debt based on the fact that we were obsessed with making sure that we had all our own photos—if you saw a photo of Modest Mouse in *DIW*, you didn't see it anywhere else." It was a great idea while it lasted, and the fiscal concerns didn't seem to affect Hawthorne's commitment to image quality. "When I'd pick up magazines of our competitors," Hawthorne says, "and I saw a lot of promo photos, it just looked a little lazy. I didn't want any page of *DIW* to look lazy. The photos always played a really big role." Ellenby, as photo editor, dealt with the photos for three years before stepping down to make time for other projects.

Matmos 2003

The Velvet Teen 2002

Rilo Kiley 2001

Rogue Wave 2004

Queens of the Stone Age 1999

Greg Dulli 2000

The Work

"Probably 90 percent of my work is 35 mm," says Ellenby. "I also have a medium-format Pentax. But I *really* love these cheap plastic cameras from China called Holgas." Holgas were developed in 1982 as an inexpensive, bare bones way to shoot medium-format film. "The Holga's all plastic, even the lens," says Ellenby, "and they leak light like crazy and don't wind the film well, so you get all these crazy flares, light flares, all over the film." Almost all of the shots in this book that may appear to have been doctored were in fact shot with a Holga. "There are only a few pictures in the book that were doctored on the computer. One is the Pinback photo," explains Ellenby. "I just took two 35 mm negatives and put them together on the computer to create the composition. But all the other stuff, like those long strips, those are all just natural, straight off the film."

Ellenby continues, "Most cameras, when you fire the shutter you have to advance the film. But this thing you can just hit the shutter as many times as you want without advancing the film, or you can hit the shutter while you're advancing the film, stretch out people's heads. It's a really fun camera. Sometimes you open it and find the film hasn't wound up. Medium-format film is not in a container like 35 mm; it winds onto another spool and it's got a paper back with a coating to protect it from the light. And when it doesn't wind properly, light's leaking in from the ends." With the Holga, no two shots are alike, and that's why photographers looking for happy accidents, like Ellenby, use them.

Pinback 2001

American Analog Set 2001

John Doe 2005

John Vanderslice 2001

Imperial Teen 2002

Ben Lee 2003

Nada Surf 2005

Oranger 2005

Chuck Prophet 2004

Film School 2005

The Court & Spark 2005

Left top:
From Satellite 2004

Left bottom:
Smoosh 2005

Fog 2003

Dan the Automator 2006

John Vanderslice 2001

In-Camera Effects

Ellenby prefers not to use Photoshop at all, if he can help it. He's just not that interested in using computers to manipulate his photographs. For a tech-savvy guy with a computer-scientist father, Ellenby's approach to photography is pretty lo-fi. "Pretty much all of my work is in-camera," he says. "I mean, I do adjust the color levels a teeny bit on the computer, you know. But I'm not going to take an image and totally change its color too much. It also depends on the shot; sometimes you have to do more and sometimes you do less, but most of the time it's pretty much right off the film. And there's things you can do like cross-processing, which is processing slide film in print chemicals or vice-versa to get interesting-looking tones in photos. There's an Actionslacks photo (right) that's a cross-process picture, and it has really weird greens and stuff like that. That was print film processed in slide chemicals, so you end up with a color transparency. Mostly it's trial and error. You just take a lot of photos and see what works."

Fiver 2000

764-Hero 2000

The Flipsides 2002

Sebadoh 1998

Portraits

Portraits of musicians perform double duty. In the first place, they're taken for promotional reasons—the shots appear in magazine articles, press packets, Web sites, and the like. Promo materials simply look flimsy without them, and the brain seems to need a visual image to wrap itself around a band. It's far easier to remember a band once you've seen the picture, isn't it? But in the process of promoting the band—advertising it, if you will—these photos can and should reveal something of the genuine character of a band or artist: People often make snap judgements about a band on the strength of those photos without ever having heard a note. They let you know whether the music is coming from a collection of dudes with tidy soul patches and matching paper jumpsuits or four regular guys who dress like your friends. Photos provide clues to what kind of neighborhood they come from or whether they have a sense of humor. The truth is, you can often rightly predict a great deal about the values of a band or artist or even what the music will sound like from looking at the photo.

Ellenby once had the honor of shooting a portrait of John Lee Hooker. "It was just a couple years before he passed," Ellenby says, "so he was very old and very frail. Shaking his hand—and he'd also been playing guitar since he was around four years old—his hand felt like it had no bones in it. It was all supple and leathery. I'd say he was nice." As usual, Ellenby didn't get much time to shoot: "The publicist said, 'Okay, when you start shooting you can shoot for five minutes.' But that's cool with me, because I actually really enjoy working quickly. I don't like treating bands like models. I like to just get them out in front of the camera and get going. Even if we're in the studio, we just get right to work. I figure out what the shoot's going to be like way beforehand, get the cameras and everything else ready, and just do it. Ten minutes is not uncommon. If it lasts more than an hour it's kind of a long one."

Beyond taking a compelling, excellent picture, a huge challenge for the music photographer is developing a concept for each

"The first thing I'll think is, what kind of musician is this? Like for a blues artist like John Lee Hooker—I haven't shot too many blues artists, he's probably the only one I've ever shot—you want it to be a little bit dark and gritty. So I shot really fast film, black-and-white. Also because I didn't know where he was going to be, or what the situation was going to be like, and figured he probably wouldn't appreciate me hitting him with a flash. The guy's in his eighties. So I had to be ready to shoot in a low-light situation.

"I get the film ready—it's T-MAX 3200, and I usually shoot it at 1600, so it's a one-stop pull for all you photo geeks out there." Unlike many photographers, Ellenby

doesn't shoot Polaroids, which means he won't see the film until it returns from the lab. "I kind of have the image in my head, and when I get a picture back from the lab, I think I know what it's going to look like. But sometimes it's still a surprise to me. I just like getting down to work—shoot the film and trust that my instincts are going to be good enough to get some good stuff. There are times when the work isn't as strong as you'd like it to be, but I think in any discipline, that's going to happen. And you just don't show people all your photos. I'm sure the musicians I've shot in my career have only shared with us about 20 percent of their output. You can't be 'on' all the time. I probably average about four to ten shots a roll that I think are pretty kickass, and I think that's pretty good. Because really, your job is not to document the whole day—here's John Lee Hooker getting up and having breakfast, eating with his grandchildren—you're there to shoot an editorial image, to show him, get a mood of him across to his fans. You're going to have one picture, maybe two or three, depending on the piece. So you just have to focus on getting that one thing done. I may shoot a whole roll, but if I only have five minutes, I can't do too many different things, so the pictures are all pretty similar; I just move around a little bit to try to get the expression on his face just right, and then I'm done."

It's a whole hell of a lot trickier than it sounds to capture who the band or artist really is, otherwise there'd be a million great photographers. Peter Ellenby has a way of making just about everyone comfortable in his presence, which pays off for both Ellenby and the artists. Mark Eitzel, the sad-eyed lead singer and songwriter of American Music Club, says, "Peter was a great photographer for AMC—he understood the music. He was one of us. We felt really comfortable during the sessions and loved the results."

Eitzel's is merely one voice in a thousand. John Vanderslice, former mastermind behind MK Ultra and current solo artist, owner of Tiny Telephone recording studio, and all-around nice guy, remembers his first shoot with Ellenby. "My old band, MK Ultra, called him up," recalls Vanderslice. "He lived in the same place he's living now, right near the 280 overpass, and he said, 'Just come to my place and we'll fool around.' We were all wearing suits, and he said, 'Oh yeah, stand on this overpass.'" Dan Carr, itinerant bass player and former or current member of MK Ultra, Preston School of Industry, Creeper Lagoon, and the Court & Spark, among others, refers to the era as "the dapper days. We were all very nattily dressed." Vanderslice continues, "I swear to God he took, like, five photos. It was over in three minutes."

Ellenby took a handful of shots in a few minutes, which didn't initially impress Vanderslice: "I

thought, there's no way these are gonna turn out, you know what I mean? I was kind of under-whelmed with the process. I just assumed that when you had band photos it was some incredibly intense experience and you were pushed to the limits of your ability to look interesting. Because I didn't think we had it in us to stand and stay put and be exciting, you know?" For his part, Carr recalls being pretty happy it was a fast shoot: "If you look, three of us have cups of coffee beside us because we were freezing our asses off that night."

"A couple of days later, Peter called me up," Vanderslice contin-ues, "and said, 'You should come over and check these out.' One of the photos on that overpass, a shot where we're kind of leaning on each other . . . I could not believe, just from a technical standpoint, how beautiful it was. I mean, it was just gorgeous. And you know, from that point on I was like, 'This guy is the shit.' "

DIW's Marc Hawthorne says he only got to see Ellenby shooting portraits once, but the experience stayed with him. "Ninety-nine percent of the time I wasn't at photo shoots, but the one time I was there I really saw Ellenby's low-key charm in action," he explains. "I actually did the interview with Marine Research from England, which is the band that sort of emerged from Heavenly after their guitar player killed himself. They were playing at Bottom of the Hill and they went to Peter's place

to take the photos, and just for timing issues I did the interview there. There were five people in the band; Peter brought the ingredients for tuna fish sandwiches. So the whole thing was each one of them preparing part of the tuna fish sandwich, and the final photo is the entire band eating tuna fish sandwiches. The atmosphere there at Peter's became really nice and friendly and not intimidating at all. He probably didn't know the band, but it was a great idea to have them be active and doing something, and they were all really eager to do it. Complete strangers from different countries instantly became fast friends for a few hours. I'm sure bands like Coldplay and U2 are so used to photo sessions that they just go in there and make their pose and whatever, they're done. Whereas when you're working with indie rock bands, as Peter always has, it seems way more difficult because you often have really self-conscious people who aren't used to being photographed and don't know how it works. I'm sure half the art of taking portraits of rock bands is being able to get them to feel comfortable."

Bob Reed and Mike Drake recall one such particularly comfortable album cover shoot with Ellenby. "He shot the cover of Overwhelming Colorfast's *Moonlight and Castanets* album in his bedroom," says Reed. He pauses to smoke for a second. "A lot of people have rules, house rules—when you walk in the house, please take your

shoes off—that kind of thing. We got there and he told us he had this house rule." Drake chimes in, "'Please take your pants off.'" Bob concurs. "'Take your pants off before you come into the bedroom.' That was the rule. So we did the photo shoot for the album cover with no pants." Drake looks at Reed sideways for a moment. "It really captured the vibe of the record, though," he says. "It did, it did," affirms Reed. "It was uncomfortable at first, but after a couple of martinis we were in the moment."

Zach Rogue of Rogue Wave has been photographed by Ellenby a few times for various publications. "My favorite time working with him was when we did some pictures for the 2005 Noise Pop Festival,"

Rogue remembers. "They were putting us on the cover of the program guide. We did it at his place, his apartment, and he had a really cool kind of design concept he'd put together. When we walked in, he said, 'Why don't you put on Jeanné [Ellenby, Peter's wife]'s jacket?' Immediately I was like, 'I have no ego.' [Laughs.] And you know, that's the point, realizing that. Everyone goes through head trips when they see pictures of themselves, but there's no need. I was holding this stuffed penguin half the time, and that, to me, was more enjoyable and more interesting. Just stuff that allows you to loosen up a little bit and realize that it's just an aperture you're looking into. It was just very easy, natural. We watched *Heavy Metal Parking Lot* after the shoot was over."

Previous spread and left:

American Music Club 2004

Cisco the Frisco Mack 1995

Dashboard Confessional 2001

Matt Nathanson 2000

Mike Watt 1998

John Lee Hooker 1999

Jolly 1999

Mark Kozelek,
Red House Painters 2000

Rogue Wave 2005

MK Ultra 1997

Grandaddy 1999

Chuck Prophet 2004

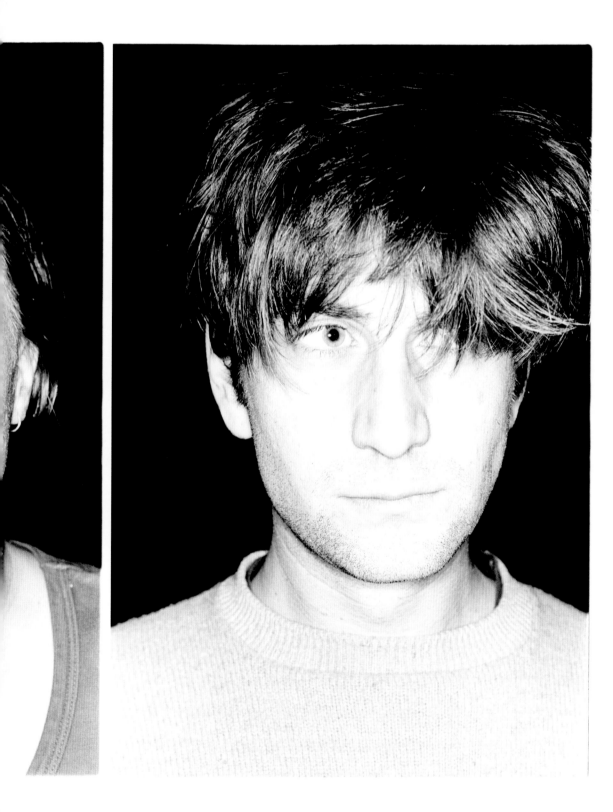

Unwound 2001

The Promise Ring 1999

Built to Spill 1997

Aaron Nudelman 2000

Spiral Stairs, Preston School of Industry 2001

Bright Eyes 2000

Bob Mould 2005

The Knitters (and friend) 1999

The Get Up Kids 1999

Les Claypool 2003

Phil Crumar 2000

John Doe 1998

John Doe 2002

David Kilgour, The Clean 2001

Dominique Durand, Ivy 2001

The Rise 1989

Shooting the Author

San Francisco author Beth Lisick remembers her experience getting photographed by Ellenby for some promo or other:

I needed a picture when my second book came out. I had seen Peter's pictures everywhere, and I knew I didn't want a cheesy author photo. So I called him up and he was really cool about it. I went over to his place and we just hit it off immediately. He was raised in the Bay Area and so was I. And we actually knew some people in common—besides San Francisco people, like people from Palo Alto, San Jose, and stuff. We took some pictures in the studio first, I think. Then we just hung out and talked, and then we went for a walk, we just went walking around Dogpatch. It was really windy, I remember that. It was a really nice day, a Saturday afternoon, and we just went around and looked at stuff. We had no agenda beyond shooting a picture. We were just spending the afternoon together. It was really fun. And just that thing when you're with somebody you've never met before but you just get a nice feeling from them, and you can just talk and it seems very normal. So we had a great time. We took a bunch of pictures while we were walking around, and then we were kind of done, and we knew we were done, but we cracked open some beers and watched the deleted scenes from *Spinal Tap.* It was really funny and it was really nice.

This was a pretty unusual photo shoot for Lisick. "For me, and I think for a lot of people, it's a really vulnerable thing to get your picture taken because you feel so self-conscious," she says. "And I think I did feel weird at first, but then it turned fun. Yeah, so it was nice. It was sort of like, I don't know, cuddling after you have sex, you know? We were drinking beers and watching *Spinal Tap.* I didn't have to leave right away. I didn't have to get out of bed, you know? It was great. We just hung out for a while. And like I said, it was the first day I'd met him."

The photo Ellenby picked as his favorite from that day isn't the one Lisick used for her promo materials, but it is the one in this book. She explains: "I would never have used that photo, you know? It's not a way that I would choose to portray myself, but obviously it's me and it's part of me, and he picked it. I was kind of like, Wow, cool: I didn't think there was anybody who could take a sexy photo of me that I wouldn't feel completely weird about. So it was funny."

Another interesting element of Ellenby's portraiture may not be obvious in any given photo, but if you look at a series of portraits, you start to notice a thread that's uncommon in rock photography: people are smiling. The smiles are never forced—he would never pull a "Say cheese!" moment, except as a joke, and people feel that from him immediately. The smiles and laughter come from genuine happiness, when people feel comfortable and lose their self-consciousness in front of Ellenby's lens. Lisick notes this trend, as well: "People smile for him and look natural. That's always something that you want, to try to capture the heart of somebody. But I think in band situations, you can totally get into that weird, fronting-posing thing. It's really interesting that a lot of people use Peter's photos as their band photos, because [a formal photo shoot] is usually where people are really trying hard to project some image or something like that. But somehow he gets who they are."

"Peter's photos have got a gritty, honest thing going on," explains

Dan Carr. "No one's dressed up in clothes that they wouldn't wear, no one's posed in weird poses in front of a table full of liquor bottles and piles of coke and chicks. I mean, you're not going to see a picture of Built to Spill in front of a limousine, because that's not who they are. At no point does he try to make his subjects be anything other than what they just would be. He puts you at ease so you're not thinking about it. You're talking with your buddy, then all of a sudden, boom boom, he's snapping pictures and you're not really paying attention. That's an obvious thing, but I don't think everybody has the skill to put people at ease, or else everyone would be a good photographer. I think that's a rare skill."

Beth Lisick 2001

Shooting Live

Ellenby's approach to shooting live music is freewheeling and entirely unconstrained. You can usually find him down front, pounding his head and throwing horns with the rest of them, singing along to all the songs. And then when the time is right, or when he knows the band is working toward a rock-and-roll moment—the singer in the air, feet splayed back so far that you think he's gotta fall on his knees, at the very least—Peter will set his beer down, pull his camera out of his jacket pocket, tear his eyes away from the band to set stop, shutter speed, and focus, and then lift his arm and start snapping pictures.

"He is first and foremost a fan," says Bob Reed. "Every time I've ever seen him in the crowd he's been rocking out and having a good time. He's there initially as a fan, and that's what I think really translates into his photography."

Ellenby's photographs put you in the audience, at the show, and very nearly buy you a beer. They are feverish, exhilarating, fucked up—just like how you might feel at a rock show, working on your fourth beer, buzzed from the crowd and the bands, ears ringing from dangerously loud music, lights dimmed and colored so it feels like a party.

"Peter is the guy who's at every show," explains Mike Drake, now guitarist and singer for Oranger, "holding the camera over his head, sticking it in the face of the band and waving it around. For a while I didn't think he was taking pictures. One time I had him show me his technique. And he says, 'Like this.'" Drake waves a straight arm seemingly indiscriminately around in the air above his head. "I said, 'Oh, I've seen you do that a bunch of times. I didn't know you were shooting.'"

Drake continues, "You don't even notice that he's taking pic-tures, even if you're in the audi-ence, because he's rocking out. All his pictures have such motion— he's not trying to hold the camera steady, or get the right lighting balance and all that. It's all energy, he's trying to capture energy."

Take the photo of Sonic Youth's Thurston Moore—he leans back at a precarious angle, only partly in focus, and you can feel the pools of feedback rolling out of his guitar; a flare or two dirties the lens and a band of black fog obscures the bottom of the shot. Or Frank Black, who looms large in the frame, shot blindly while Ellenby was smashed against the stage below. You might get sweat in your eye just looking at them. As much as photos can and do document real events and real people, they are not objective, sterile, uninflected images. They are subjective distortions of reality, even if their aim is honesty. It is, in effect, lying to tell the truth.

Ellenby's subjects and his camera are on the move. Arms, heads, guitars, hair, fingers, hands, mouths, legs, feet, teeth, and tongues all blur and skip across the frame. He talks about a photo being a frozen moment in time, but it's as if one still, frozen moment is unable to contain all the energy and passion in one of his live shots, so the shutter, or the eye, must stay open just a little longer to take it all in. Lights burn brighter, leaving glowing trails, and movement blurs, reflecting speed and force in its range. It's a little hallucinatory.

Matt Jervis has known Peter Ellenby for at least fifteen years. Jervis, the front man for Kingdom First and Clarke Nova, now puts his energy into graphic art and designing rock posters. "Peter's scrappy," says Jervis with a twinkle in his eye, "that's the first thing that comes to mind. And he kind of reminds me of that guy who basically documented the Seattle scene. He's like our Charles Peterson.

"If you really want a taste of Peter Ellenby," muses Jervis, "it's the live stuff that really put him on the map as far as being an important photographer. The live stuff, you can smell the smoke and that kind of shit. Like catching [Tim] Scanlin [of Actionslacks] in the air . . . because he's right there, he's gravitating toward this energy, and his lens is this magnet. And the fish-eye pulls it further. He knows when the singer hits the chorus. Having known the band, he knows the singer falls down at this point, and he's there: he's got the shot."

Jervis suggests that when the bands know Ellenby's there, they play it up for him. "It's like you're goofing off for Peter," he says. "He's there, he's screaming with a kilt on or something, and he's taking photos, and you're fucking around and having a good time with someone you know. I think a lot of the time his best results come when he's not trying to be covert. It's an energy that goes back and forth. So a lot of times the best live shows are when the band is playing for Peter, because they're just having fun with it. And that's an intimacy that a lot of photographers are trying to get. The subtext, that intimacy, that opening up thing. Everyone wants to crack the subject open and get the shot that no one ever did."

The Murder City Devils 1999

Previous page, clockwise:

1 **Imperial Teen** 1996
2 **Red 5** 1996
3 **Actionslacks** 1996
4 **Brainiac** 1996
5 **Modest Mouse** 1996
6 **Kingdom First** 1998
7 **Red Aunts** 1995
8 **The Wedding Present** 1996

Rocket from the Crypt 1999

Built to Spill 2003

Sonic Youth 2003

Frank Black 1998

Harvey Danger 1998

Overwhelming Colorfast 1997

MK Ultra 1998

Death Star 1997

Previous spread, left to right:

Jeremy Enigk 1997
Archers of Loaf 1997
Knapsack 1998
Beulah 1999

Supersuckers 1996

Previous spread:

Foo Fighters 1996

Spoon 1997

American Analog Set 1997

Swirl Happy 1996

Mensclub 1996

Jon Spencer Blues Explosion 1996

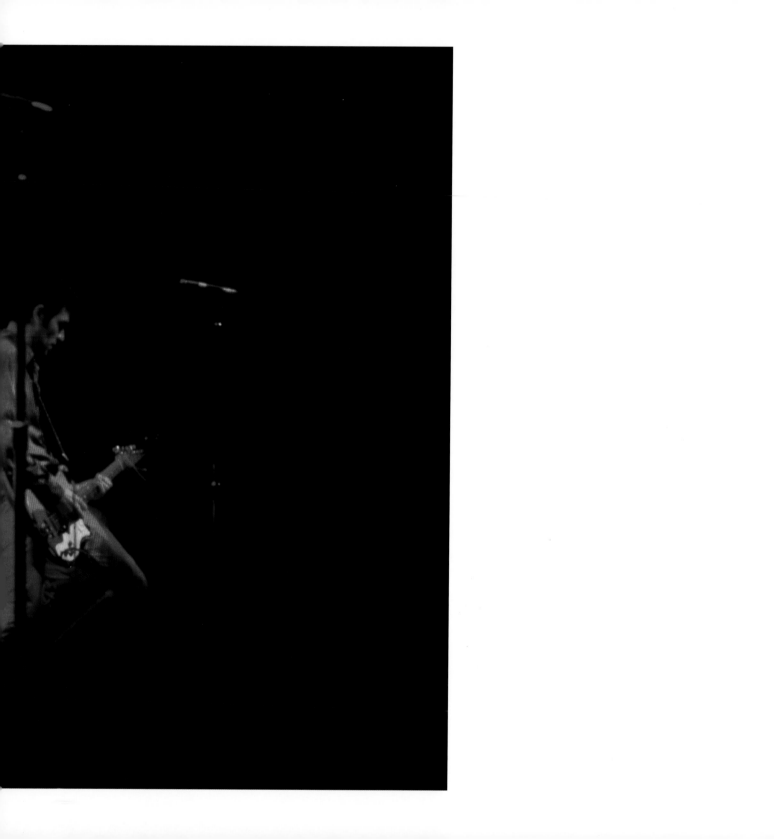

Paul Rigby, Neko Case, and John Doe 2002

Left:
Chixdiggit 1996

Right:
Calvin Krime 1997

Left to right:

Kenickie 2001
764-Hero 1996
Fuck 1998

Henry's Dress 1997

Meices 1996

The Muffs 1997

Engine 88 1995

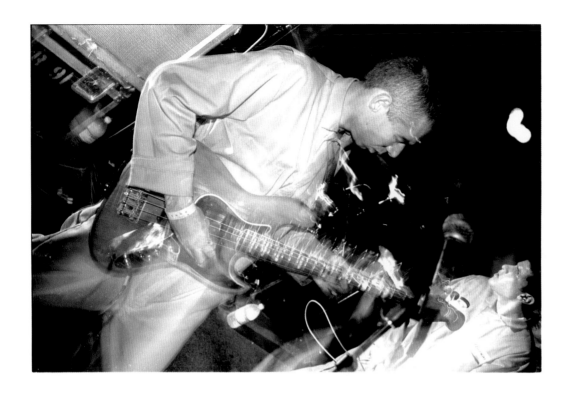

Beastie Boys 1998

Spearhead 1994

Uncle Joe's Big Ol' Driver 1995

Jesus Lizard

Ellenby talks about shooting the Jesus Lizard at the Bottom of the Hill:

When the Jesus Lizard came to play an anniversary show at the Bottom of the Hill, Ramona [Downey] and Kathleen [Owen] wanted to be sure I came down to shoot the show. It was a super show, and I got a great portrait of the band. It was David Yow's birthday and he was totally bombed out of his mind, he was just wrecked. Having the greatest day ever. The portrait is really cool—he's prying his eye open, looking in the camera's fisheye. The show was totally rockin' and hilarious. He had about a fifty-foot-long mic cable, because he likes to go crowd surfing. He's not Sammy Hagar, so he didn't have the sweet wireless setup. He cruised out, getting crowd surfed all the way to the bar. Then he jumped behind the bar and grabbed all the money from the cash register and stuffed it in his pockets. Ramona was like, "HEY! Whaddya doing?!" She ran out to him, chased him down, and grabbed all the money back.

The Jesus Lizard 1998

Coda

What is the elusive thing, the special element, that changes a technically interesting picture into a great one? Maybe it's humanity and honesty, or a sense of humor, or an eye that transcends framing and can see and imagine in multiple ways simultaneously. Whatever it is, Matt Jervis thinks he knows why Peter has it. "The people who can capture the subject best are the people who have an intimate relationship with it," he suggests. "I think Peter really knows music, and that comes naturally, and that's what works."

Beth Lisick has a slightly different take. "I think there's a sweetness to [Peter's approach]," she says. "Like the portraits—not necessarily the live shots—I think that everybody looks kind of sweet in his pictures. Because people are comfortable with him, their defenses aren't up, they aren't really pose-y or doing things you see in typical 'rock' photos."

At the end of the day, in spite of the ever-present camera, it seems clear the people in Ellenby's life will remember the man more than the photographer. "Peter's one of those guys who has a heart of gold," says Kevin Arnold. "He's just a really genuine, caring, giving guy. He's one of those friends where you never feel like you give enough back to him." Matt Jervis agrees: "Peter's such a likeable guy. He's a guy who's got a hell of a lot of friends. He just has that kind of personality."

Clockwise:

Grandaddy 1997
Swell 1996
764-Hero 1997
Melvins 1997

Peter 2003
photo by Jeanné Ellenby